COURAGE
FOR THE REST OF US

COURAGE
FOR THE REST OF US

Going From Ordinary To Extraordinary

JIM ESCHRICH

New York

Courage For The Rest of Us

Going From Ordinary to Extraordinary

Cover Design by 3 Dog Design: www.3dogdesign.com

ISBN 978-1-60037-687-0

Library of Congress Control Number: 2009932816

MORGAN · JAMES
THE ENTREPRENEURIAL PUBLISHER

Morgan James Publishing, LLC
1225 Franklin Ave., STE 325
Garden City, NY 11530-1693
Toll Free 800-485-4943
www.MorganJamesPublishing.com

In an effort to support local communities, raise awareness and funds, Morgan James Publishing donates one percent of all book sales for the life of each book to Habitat for Humanity. Get involved today, visit **www.HelpHabitatForHumanity.org.**

Contents

"It is not the critic who counts, not the man who points out how the strong man stumbled, or where the doer of deeds could have done better. The credit belongs to the man who is actually in the arena, whose face is marred by dust and sweat and blood, who strives valiantly, who errs and comes short again and again, who knows the great enthusiasms, the great devotions, and spends himself in a worthy cause, who at best knows achievement and who at the worst, if he fails, at least fails while daring greatly so that his place shall never be with those cold and timid souls who know neither victory or defeat."

— Teddy Roosevelt

1
A Surreal Experience

"Oh, yeah, just one little draw back to this delightful
winter sport. The high speed crash. Always remember,
your bones will not break in bobsled.
No, no, no. They shatter."
— Irv, in the movie *Cool Runnings*

It's about ten minutes before the race and I'm in my own little world atop this mountain. Each of the team members are in their own little worlds as well, our pilot, brakeman, and the other pusher. We've just finished warming up and are making last minute preparations to enter the track with our sled. I don't know what the rest of my team is thinking, but me; I'm still taking it all in. I can't believe I'm actually here in Winterberg, Germany, for a whole month, nestled in the German countryside north of the Alps as a member of the U.S. National Bobsled Team. Because I was an alternate, I didn't make the initial trip with the rest of the team to Germany. Being an alternate means you only get called when another team member gets sick or injured. Truth be told, I was so bad I was an alternate to the alternates. Needless to say, I was stunned one morning when my roommate called and said, "Jim, someone from the Bobsled Federation called and they want you in Germany. You need to get over there ASAP!"

So, here I am, pinching myself to see if I'm dreaming. The whole experience is surreal. Glancing down the hill I see portions of the track as it snakes down towards the bottom. Spectators are beginning to line the track. Jim McKay's words from his Wide World of Sports show about *"the thrill of victory and the agony of defeat"* now resonate within me like never before. Here I am, no longer a spectator in the drama unfolding, but a fully engaged participant. The weather rounds out the idyllic picture as it is c-o-l-d—cold.

Most people talk of having butterflies fluttering in their stomachs when they are nervous. Well, the guy who came up with that dainty description must have never bobsledded! Bobsledders don't have butterflies, they have giant condors. I know I did because they were picking at my guts! These feelings come to me with good reason. Bobsledding is like a poorly maintained amusement park ride. That is to say, when things go wrong they go very, very wrong. When a sled tips over on its side the occupants' heads and shoulders are exposed to hard ice, which at 80 to 90 miles-per-hour might as well be concrete. Injuries can range from abrasions and sprains to broken bones. People can die in this sport. The sled and occupants weigh around 1500 lbs. Marry the two together, send it into a steep turn, and you're talking upwards of five times your body weight (or five G's). Fear is just something you have to deal with. But there are other fears in addition to bodily harm. There's the fear of screwing up and letting your teammates down. These are people's dreams you're dealing with, so the emotions run deep. And to cap it all off; I'm afraid of roller coasters. I always have been. Now there's one for you—a guy petrified of roller coasters on the U.S. Bobsled Team! Needless to say, I kept this little gem to myself.

Earlier that morning the dining hall had been quieter than normal. Absent was the usual animated conversation at the various tables. Loose chatter and horseplay had been replaced with quiet focus. After all the sacrifice and hard work to get to this point, you sure don't want to blow it because of lack of focus. I've tried my best to get my head screwed on straight and I believe it is, but from the moment my eyes popped open today, my nerves have been bouncing all over the place. Actually, my nerves have been in overdrive from the second I arrived here. Even during the flight over here, my emotions were all over the place—up and down, excitement, anticipation, fear, and nervous energy all bound up inside of me looking for some form of escape. And you know what? I had every reason to feel this way. One week of practice in a four-man sled was the sum total of my experience prior to my first Olympic Trials qualifying race. Yes, I was scared to death on a variety of levels.

The flight to Germany gave me plenty of time to think about the incredible path I was on. I thought about all those people who told me I'd never make it, that I was crazy to think I could pull it off, that I was just wasting my time even thinking about it.

Don't get me wrong, my critic's had a good case. Who in their right mind tries out for the U.S. Bobsled Team at age thirty? Maybe it would have made sense if I were a trained athlete with years of experience, who knew what he was doing. But I wasn't any of those things. In high school I played one sport—football, and sat the bench much of my senior year after coming down with a diagnosis of Chrone's Disease, an inflammatory bowel disease. Then, my knee got torn up in college during a pick-up game of touch football. Years later this same injury led to my medical discharge from the United States Marine Corp Officer Candidate School. I liked lifting weights, but that doesn't an athlete make. Nope, there wasn't anything spectacular about my athletic background. My bobsled teammates, well, that was an entirely different matter. Many were college football players and track athletes.

The team's pilot calls us together now. It's show time. My mouth has become like cotton as we heave the sled onto the grooves cut into the track. I shake my arms and legs vigorously while jumping up and down in a vain attempt to keep those condors in my stomach from flying right out my mouth. Everyone places their hands on top of each other's while the pilot leads us in a brief, mindless chant that's supposed to pump everyone up. Breaking out of the huddle we each retreat to our own respective spots alongside or behind the sled. My senses are dancing now. I'm a live wire. Nervousness, excitement, and fear are all surging through my system.

Now, like sprinters in the blocks, we wait. The tension can be sliced. Countdown can't come soon enough. Each team member grabs the handle along the sled that they'll use to push against. Collectively we crunch our bodies down low preparing to explode when the time comes. Everything must be done in sync. I grip and re-grip the handle like it will make some sort of difference, but it doesn't.

The track is clear. We get the green light and the rocking begins. The bobsled gently sways back and fourth, back and fourth, until that perfect rhythm is found and then the count begins. One, two, and on the count of three we explode into the handles, driving through our hips with all the power we can muster.

My spikes are digging in, kicking up ice, and my knees are driving up and down like pistons in an engine. The world around me is a blur. The track begins to pitch down steeply so the sled is picking up serious speed. We have thirty to forty meters to push the sled as fast as we can before jumping in, so we're in an all out sprint. The push is critical. Every tenth of a second gained here translates into the three-tenths at the finish. The pilot jumps into the sled and I know my turn is coming up next. The fear is replaced by a mindless urge to run, push, and grunt my way down the track. There's no time to think or reflect now, its all in the moment.

I finally reach the point where I can't run any faster. One stride too many and the sled will begin to outrun me, and that can't be good. I vault myself into the sled flinging my left leg across my body, landing my left foot on a little ledge no wider than a foot and about as long. I have to hit this ledge accurately or I'll be eating ice for the next quarter of a mile. I hit the ledge perfectly, yes! Now I push off with this foot and throw my body in behind the pilot.

Once inside the sled, I blindly search for handles and pegs to brace myself against. My limbs need a home, and quickly, or I'll be like a human pinball within the sled. And god forbid I drive my needle-like spikes into the pilot's calves and distract him from, um, other duties like driving the damn sled down the track!

As I brace myself in the sled, I lower my profile to reduce drag, every little bit helps. My job is done. For better or worse, I'm now just along for the ride. Whether we succeed or fail at this point depends on the pilot. We're rocketing down the track now and I'm staring at the little pieces of ice vibrating on the bottom of the sled. The sound inside the sled is that of a loud rumble. The rumble gets louder and louder as the sled gathers momentum. As we wiz by, I hear the crowd cheering us on. My body leans in and out of the turns. My shoulders ache. I'm hunched over and the guy's helmet behind me is smashing into my spine. A big turn is coming, and before I can take a breath, WHAM, we're into it. My body is being pushed down with the force of several times my body weight. It feels like the sled, and I, is going to break in half.

Two years earlier I was lying in bed staring up at the ceiling terrified—terrified at where my life was and terrified at where it was going. I was twenty-nine, unmarried, with no prospects, and no sense of direction. Most of my friends had families and were settled into their careers. They were doing the safe and expected things. I was trying my hand at safe and expected, but wasn't having much luck.

I knew lying there that I had to take my life in a different direction. I wanted to feel passionate about something, anything, but what? Then a thought came to me. I remembered hearing Jim McKay's voice broadcasting from the Lake Placid Winter Olympic games. Lake Placid was only a few hours away from where I was living at the time and I got to thinking about the bobsled races that had been broadcast from there. I had always loved bobsledding. My first memory of the sport goes all the way back to the 1968 Winter Olympic Games in Grenoble, France. "I should try out for the bobsled team," I thought. As crazy as the idea sounded, the thought persisted. Now it's almost one year later and here I am experiencing something so few in the world get to do. I can't believe it.

Nearly everyone thought I was crazy when I told them I was trying out for the bobsled team. Sure, I'd get comments like, "That's nice, keep me posted." It sounded an awful like, "We don't have any open positions right now, but we'll keep your resume on file." Nobody was taking me seriously. One friend of mine, a sensible type guy, told me point blank that I needed to grow up, that I didn't have a chance athletically, and that I'd be competing against highly trained Olympic athletes. He was right about all of it. I did need to grow up, and it certainly appeared I didn't have a snowball's chance of succeeding, but hey, what did I have to lose? My sensible friend now has a framed, autographed picture of me taken at the U.S. Olympic Bobsled Trials hanging in his office!

Our sled crosses the finish line. After about 1500 meters, nearly a mile, the run is over. The whole ride took less than a minute. My head comes up for a look around. As the brakes are applied, the sled slams back and forth against the side of the track. It hardly registers. I know nothing bad can happen to me now. We've made it. A huge sigh of relief rushes over me. We put the sled on the truck and head back up the hill for another run. As we ascend the mountain, the condors that had deserted me at the start of my descent begin to nest once again . . . and looking back, I never felt more alive.

2
Being True to Myself

"Courageous risks are life-giving, they help you grow,
make you brave, and better than you think you are."
— Joan L. Curcio

Bobsledding proved to be a pivotal moment. My entire attitude about myself and how I would move forward in the future changed. Even now as I think about it, it's strange to me that something as inane and trivial as bobsledding could have that kind of impact on my life. The nature of the challenge, however, must have been exactly what I needed at the time. What Joan L. Curcio says in the above quote is absolutely true. *"Courageous risks are life-giving, they help you grow, make you brave, and better than you think you are."*

Now, I'm certainly no expert. I'm just an ordinary guy who's learned a few things on this journey called life that I'd like to pass on. As you will find out in the coming pages, this book has nothing to do with triumphant entries into Olympic Stadiums or winning Gold medals. Nor is it a grand attempt at elevating me as some self-help guru. No, it's a book about ordinary people like you and me, being capable of extraordinary things. And it all starts with being passionate. You see, it is from our deepest passions that courage springs. Deep passion brings forth courageous action. That's where courage comes from. Courage is not an end, but a means. It's an offshoot of feeling passionate about something.

The term *courage* is derived from the Latin root *cor*, which literally means *heart* or *core*. The original use of the word *courage* meant to *stand by one's core*. Standing by one's core *is* living authentically or living true to our core self. It's here, in our center that true passion resides.

At twenty-nine years old, the prospect of sitting behind a desk was about as passionless of an existence as I could have imagined for myself. Yet, there I was just going through the motions of life while my core self, the authentic me, was slowly but surely wasting away. To live passionately, I decided a revolution was in order, and since bobsledding was the only thing on my radar that was giving me goose bumps, bobsledding it was. Trying out for the team seemed simple enough. All I had to do was go to Lake Placid, take an eight event test, pass it, and I would be on the U.S. National Bobsled Team. The test consisted of 30, 60, 100, and 300 meter sprints; five consecutive hops for distance; a vertical jump; throw a sixteen pound shot from between your knees; and clean a weight from the floor to your shoulders. Obviously, the faster you ran, the greater the distance you hopped, the further you threw the shot, and so on, the more points you were awarded. The objective was to see how explosive you were which was an important trait given the fact that you'd be pushing a several hundred pound sled from a dead stop.

The first time I tried out I failed miserably, falling hundreds of points short of the six hundred and fifty point minimum required. I was so bad, it was embarrassing. It was at this point I think I officially hit bottom. "Maybe all those naysayers were right," I thought. "Maybe it *was* crazy to think I could do this on a whim." But, one thing I've learned is if there is a blessing in hitting bottom it's that you finally have something to push off of. It was either push off or stay defeated on the bottom. Fortunately, I chose the former and decided to give it another shot, only this time I was determined to learn from my past failures and prepare myself like never before. I trained hard and I trained smart. I sprinted. I lifted. I found myself a track and a weight lifting coach. I practiced the events contained in the test and even hired a sports psychologist to help wring out of me the last few drops of whatever potential I had. No stone was left unturned. Coming back to Lake Placid the second time around I was well-prepared and confident. And two days after the testing began, the results were in. I had made the team by a whopping one point! That's right, one single point. Now maybe it's clear why I said earlier that I was an alternate to the alternates. You could not have made the team with fewer points than I had. Still, I had shown great improvement and regardless of how close it was, I had made the U.S. National Bobsled Team.

In the days that followed, however, it was apparent that my victory was a hollow one. Being at the shallow end of the athletic pool that made up the National Team, I was not exactly in high demand for one of the individual teams (USA I, USA II, etc.). Basically, if one of the teams needed me they would call me, otherwise, well; I was (shit?) out of luck. Nope, to make it to the Olympic Trials, much less the Olympic Games, half the members of the National Team would have had to go AWOL. . . Yeah, not likely is right. So, with those odds facing me, the rest of the National Team left for the Olympic Trials held in Winterberg, Germany. Once the team was over there, it would be a month long affair consisting of plenty of practice runs, and on weekends, qualifying runs to figure out which teams would be representing the United States at the 1988 Calgary Winter Olympic Games.

Disappointed in being left behind, I took solace in knowing I had technically made the team, having shown the greatest single year improvement in a test score of anyone on the team. With that, I started the process of letting go of my Olympic dream. Then, one morning, a few days after the National Team had left, I received a call from my roommate telling me the Bobsled Federation had called and said they needed me to get to Germany ASAP. There had been an injury on one of the teams and I was going to get my opportunity to go the Olympic Trials after all. I was stunned. "What happened to all the other alternates," I asked myself? I pondered that for a whole second before deciding I did not care!

It's funny, but in doing research for this book I came across a quote from Mark Twain that captured some of what had put me on the path I was on. He said, *"All you need in life is ignorance and confidence, and then success is sure."* If this were true I most certainly would have been a very successful man by this point in my life. I'd always been willing to try things, a lot out of ignorance and misplaced confidence. If someone was going to beat me at something they had to show me first before I would believe it. Not an all together bad trait mind you. Hell, it gave me the chutzpah to try out for the National Team when everybody said I didn't have a chance in hell of succeeding. But by itself that was never enough. It wasn't until I married ignorance and confidence with preparation that things started to come together for me. Henry Hartman summed up the piece I was missing when he said, *"Success happens when preparation meets opportunity."*

Ultimately, I failed to make it to the Olympics. Race after race my team fell hundredths of a second short which might as well have been whole seconds. I was disappointed, yet while flying back home I realized I wasn't the same person who'd arrived in Germany just weeks before. You can't come out of nowhere to make the National Bobsled Team, go to the Olympic Trials, and not have it leave an indelible mark on you. Dramatic and intense experiences are like that. I had just lived a dream. What other dreams could I make come true? I didn't know the answer, but I couldn't wait to find out.

In the years following my return from bobsledding in Winterberg, I became a single engine flight instructor and commercial rated glider pilot. These had been childhood dreams of mine. My first three entries in my logbook, in fact, were in 1972 when I was only fifteen years old. I became an entrepreneur, opening my own home based market research business. This, in turn, allowed me to be a stay-at-home dad for my kids after school—another dream. Growing up, I can remember telling my mom and dad that someday I wanted to take a year off from my job to raise my kids. I didn't do that, but being home after school for them was close enough. I purchased a few duplexes. A surprising move for me considering I am not all that handy, but hey, after bobsledding, I knew I could figure it out. I took up karate in my forties, eventually becoming a Brown Belt, and then took up snowboarding. I had taken skiing lessons as a kid, but didn't stick with it and had always regretted it. So, in my late forties, I set out, once again on another adventure and learned to snowboard. And I did other things that inspired me;

including becoming scuba qualified, a certified personal trainer, and running with the bulls in Pamplona, Spain. Most recently, I've learned how to row. Basically, thanks to my bobsled experience, I became my own little dream maker. If something had once inspired me, I tried to find a way to make it happen. Hands down, the best of my experiences is the one that gave me the courage to strike out on my own, which in turn, allowed me to be there for my girls. I am not a perfect father by any means, but being there for them after school and whenever they need me most, sure has made up for whatever shortcomings I may have.

Now, you might be thinking to yourself, *"Sure, dramatic and intense moments can be life changing, but those kinds of opportunities are rare."* And you know what, you're right. Those kinds of opportunities are rare. That's why we must seize the moment. But you know, those more frequent, simple moments can also be profound and just as life-changing.

Back when I was in the third grade, I had a classmate named Robert. He was one of those kids who arrived at school everyday looking a tad disheveled, and smelling it, too. Back then he was just considered unlucky, today he'd be considered abused and neglected. I had noticed that when we went to lunch, Robert often had nothing to eat. Back then kids brought their lunches to school. Anyway, when I mentioned this to my mom, she, without any debate or fanfare, went about packing lunches for me to bring to him. It's funny, while I have long forgotten my other classmates that year, I've never forgotten Robert.

Now, fast-forward forty years and I'm driving through the parking lot of my daughter's elementary school. The school nurse is directing traffic and she waves me through the intersection. As I moved forward, another parent, oblivious to my entry into the intersection, almost walks right into the side of my car. Mad, he slams his hand against the side of my car. Equally mad, I stop the car, get out, and we exchange our, um, differences of opinion. Nothing particularly nasty or loud, but for my daughter in the car it was uncomfortable. So much so I could tell right away she wasn't too pleased with me. When I asked her why, she told me it was because the whole affair occurred in front of her school nurse. She was embarrassed. So, I asked my daughter, *"What would you like me to do... apologize?"* I received a shrug of the shoulders and knew instantly what I had to do. I turned the car around and headed back to the school where, in front of my daughter, I apologized to the nurse for my earlier behavior. I only bring this up because months later my daughter's third grade teacher approached me and said my daughter did something that no other child had done in her thirty-some-years of teaching. She had asked her if she could stand up and address the whole class. Apparently, some of the kids were being especially mean to one another and she wanted it to stop. Yes, even small acts of courage can change you. And here's the really good news: courage begets more courage. Best-selling author and philosopher Mary Daly put it this way, *"I think you guard against decay, in general, and stagnation, by moving, by continuing to move. And with courage . . . it's a habit, a virtue; you get by courageous acts. It's like you learn to swim by swimming. You learn courage by couraging."*

Celebrate your courageous moments, big and small, and watch how they change you.

3
It's About the Passion

*"Courage is learned in the moment that you
take a leap of faith and take action."*
— Cherie Carter-Scott, Ph.D.

What gets us to act courageously and take that first step? What gets us to take that *"leap of faith and take action"* that Cherie Carter-Scott referred to above? For me, it's believing in something, and most important of all, believing in it passionately! Courage leads us to do incredible things, things oftentimes so fantastic, so unbelievable that it leaves us speechless. Without passion however, *it* just sits there like a car in park. You can rev the engine all you want, but as long as the car is in park, you're not going anywhere. And what gets you out of park and puts you into motion? A destination—a destination you have a passion for. Passion is the birthplace of courage. Passion for me is about being adventurous and trying lots of things. Doing what no one expects me to do, or better yet, thinks I can't do.

Prior to bobsledding I lived much of my adult life in black and white. I was anchored to others expectations of me. It hadn't always been this way. As a young kid I remember sitting around with a bunch of my friends, each of us taking our turn talking about the professional sport we wanted to play when we grew up. My friends mentioned baseball player, football player, etc. When it came my turn, I said something to the effect that I wanted to play *all* those sports. I wanted to be Bo Jackson before there was Bo Jackson. For those who can't remember, in the 1980's Bo Jackson was one of the most talented athletes in the world and was a multi-sport professional. Nike did a series of commercials built around the theme *'Bo knows…'* The commercials showed him in different scenes, each time in a different sport's uniform and the caption would be *"Bo knows basketball"* or *"Bo knows football"* or *"Bo knows golf"* and so on. That was truly my mindset. Then, somewhere along my way from childhood to a young man, I made the calculation that I needed to become a one-sport guy. In short, I needed to become like everyone else.

It wasn't until years later, until that morning in Syracuse, NY, when I woke up thinking about what a disappointment my life had been that I said, *"Screw this!"* Conforming or fitting in wasn't cutting it for me. So I pulled anchor and dropped it dead center on the sport of bobsledding. For one year I lived as passionately as I ever had. I felt truly alive. Everything I did had a purpose. Nothing was taken for granted. And living this way, just once, changed me forever. I was committed to living passionately. Sure, it takes some courage to live this way, but not as much as you might think. When your passion is engaged you're not preoccupied with the danger, the fear or the pain, but you're focused on the destination, the goal. Everything else becomes a sideshow.

Take my passion for flying. I was still a student pilot when my flight instructor told me to fly to an especially high altitude. I should have known something was up as my instructor was quite the character. When we got to the altitude he wanted, he then told me something I'll never forget. *"Turn the engine off,"* he said. Thinking that I had misheard, I asked if he'd repeat himself. Sure enough, that *was* what he had said. He did in fact want me to turn the engine *off.* I mean, he wanted the kind of off that involved the propeller becoming perfectly still. No simulation of an engine loss was going to cut it, no, that would have been too easy. *"Damn, what do you want me to do that for,"* I asked? He responded by saying, *"I want to make a point."* I did as I was instructed, albeit reluctantly. Needless to say, I survived. Here's my point: I didn't shut off the engine because I was especially courageous, or because I had some sort of death wish. I did it because I wanted to be a pilot and if that's what it was going to take to do it, well, that's what I was going to do. And let me add this; today there isn't a time when I hop into the cockpit of an airplane that I don't think to myself, *"Whatever happens, even if the engine stops, just keep flying the airplane!"* Point made, Mr. 'Quirky' Flight Instructor, point made.

Passion, and far less so, courage, is at the core of a well-lived life. And our passions run no deeper than when it comes to our children. While going through a divorce several years ago I was deeply concerned what it would do to them. They didn't have any say in the events that were dictated to them. Would their self-esteem plummet? Would their grades suffer? Would they withdraw? Would they grow up afraid of commitment? And how would I get along with my ex? What kind of example would we set for our children? And how would I behave as a single guy with two kids? Scary questions. And even scarier answers if you don't have a belief system that you feel passionate about. No, I'm not drifting into an Amway presentation or into a long winded religious discussion. That's not me. My kids are my passion. This is something my ex and I will always share. We may disagree, and god knows we can aggravate the hell out of one another, but at the end of the day we're both committed to doing what's right for the kids. Because of our passion for our children, we get along remarkably well. I never, and I repeat, never would have thought it possible. As I am writing this chapter, my ex's mom, sisters, and niece are in town. We've visited on a couple of occasions and even went out to dinner together. It's not unusual for one of us to be at the other's house helping out with homework. Is it always easy and carefree? Hello. We're divorced. But if getting along together is better for our girls, if it steadies them while everything else in their world is changing, well, it's worth it. We do whatever it takes. Platitudes about courage do not courage make. What you passionately believe in does. Find things to believe in. Take them to heart and let no one or anything tread on them.

My ex aside, being a single parent has been quite a ride. I didn't want to be like the dads that I sometimes see in restaurants who look like they eat all their meals there. I didn't want that for my kids. The competitor inside of me didn't want to be confined to a stereotypical role as a single father. Sure, I wanted to be a good provider, but I also wanted to be there for them after school each day. I wanted to be there to make them a snack, cook them dinner, do their laundry, and help them with their homework. When they were sick I wanted to be home with them. If I could, I wanted to be at their games, recitals, and their practices. Sure, I still needed the tone of my voice alone to mean what I say and say what I mean. Yet, my girls also needed to feel comfortable talking with me about boys, girl drama, etc. I wanted them to seek me out when they needed a hug or a shoulder to cry on. Obviously, some of these things might occur more naturally between mothers and daughters. I get that, but sharing my girls with my ex on a fifty-fifty basis, I was determined they weren't going to go without receiving at least some mom-like qualities from me. No doubt, it's taken some courage for me do these things, but what has kept me on the path that I want to follow day-in and day-out isn't courage, its passion for my girls.

It's funny, but I knew I was on the right track when my oldest daughter asked me to go to the drug store for tampons. I know, it sounds a tad weird, but for me it was a sign that I was being allowed into her teenage world. Man, was I like a proud peacock strutting into that drug store that day. (And if she reads this book in its entirety I'll probably be a dead peacock for mentioning her request, but I'll cross that bridge when I get to it.)

ভ   ভ   ভ

The desperate cry in our country today is not for more technology or education, but for things to anchor us. Our culture, our entire country for that matter, begs for things to believe in, to anchor us down and steady us through trying times.

Most of us don't vote in our elections. The ones that do, vote people into office and then don't hold them accountable for their actions (or inaction). Most of us simply sit idly by and let both extremes of the political spectrum set the tone for those of us who are in the middle. Most us watch our country's wars on television and let 'volunteers' do the fighting and sacrificing. Few of us go to church these days. We don't believe in things so passionately that we feel compelled out of principle to act, to engage into action. Life has become for many of us a spectator sport. Our unparalleled prosperity has placed us on that perch. I can't remember which Eagles' tune it was where they said, *"Every point of refuge has its price,"* but it's true. Jim Carrey, the comedic actor, said in an interview, and I'm paraphrasing here, that depressants had robbed him of his desperation that drove his creative existence. I know the same was true with me. For a while, I was on antidepressants and it took away my sense of urgency and drive. When on the medication I was very calm about everything. Too calm! Sometimes we need to be driven. Now, I'm not making a blanket statement against medication. Sometimes it is necessary. On the other hand however, we have a society that is medicated. We take a pill for everything and I'm afraid it is affecting us collectively as a society. We've lost our sense of desperation. We're so prosperous that we take things for granted and let our guard down. It's perfectly natural. Chris Rock, the comedian has a line in one of his acts that goes something like, *"We're so wealthy in this country we hunt on full stomachs."* Think about that line for a second and let it sink in. We do stuff because we can, not because we have to. What a luxury. Historically speaking, that's a relatively new phenomenon. Is it any wonder we've mismanaged things? A recession might be just what it takes for us to start living passionately again. With increased pressure and stress comes clarity. Priorities become apparent. Decisiveness returns to our vocabulary. Whoever said that necessity IS the mother of invention was spot on.

The call for passion and courage today is on so many different levels. Individually, the call is to break free from the slavery of conformity and mediocrity. Collectively, as a society, the call is to take on the challenges that lie ahead. My parent's generation survived a depression and a world war. America was built upon their courage and work ethic. They truly did whatever it took to survive and build a nation. Tom Brokaw refers to them as *The Greatest Generation,* and rightly so. What will our generation's legacy be? I don't know. But I do know that we must embrace it with passion and courage . . . and the sooner the better.

To thrive in these trying times and retain our independence in the process we must eschew the Burger King generation we've become (i.e. having everything our way) and reclaim our heritage as a passionate, courageous, disciplined, and resourceful people.

Good times or bad, one thing that makes it difficult to become passionate and courageous is that we're so plugged in electronically that it's difficult to find the time to reflect. As a consequence, too many of us are walking around on auto pilot. Professor Tom Leininger of Regis University in Denver says, *"The pace of our society in many ways makes courage difficult. You can't be courageous if you don't have a clue [of what's going on]. . ."* Unfortunately this clueless-ness that has come from being plugged in for so long carries on even when we are unplugged. Unless we are intentional about making ourselves aware we will continue to be self-absorbed and clueless.

Not only do we develop courage in ourselves by being aware of opportunities and manufacturing our own environments for growth, we develop courage in others by creating environments for growth in them. Whether it's our own children, a team, students, or a group of employees, courage is learned by giving them the opportunity to be courageous and to see courage operating in us.

The educational world is beginning to catch on to this. Michael C. Loui, Professor and Dean at the University of Illinois Urbana, noted that students need to be taught and placed in an environment that encourages the courage to take risks and learn new concepts and skills because it is only by taking reasonable risks that students learn and grow. When this happens, after graduation students would then have the self-confidence to face the unpleasant and the unknown.[1] In a study of master's degree programs, education professors Jennifer Grant Haworth of Loyola University Chicago and Clifton Conrad of Wisconsin mirrored Loui's thoughts saying:

Students who took risks within the context of a supportive learning environment . . . graduated as more competent . . . self-assured . . . imaginative and resourceful

---

1 Michael Loui, A speech at the Graduate Teacher Certificate Ceremony, April 1999; appeared in Grad Times, May/June 1999; and abridged version appeared in *College Teaching,* Summer 2006

professionals . . . [A] theater student elaborated, "One of the school's philosophies . . . is '*only by attempting the absurd can we achieve the impossible.*' And students are encouraged to do that around here. I've tried the risky things and I've failed, but it was in failing that I discovered my own voice and the impact I can have on an audience."[2]

The recession alone shouldn't be our only motivation to seek out our passions and act courageously. Business, whether it be as an owner, an employee, is becoming complex. Zurich Direct used to run a television commercial showing the outside of an urban shoe store. (I think it was a shoe store. I've tried to find the ad, but haven't had any luck.) As the business day unfolds you see the store morph into a restaurant. Everything changed. The outdoor signage changed along with the inside of the store. The only thing to remain constant was the employee who can be seen coming out of the back room tying an apron on and getting ready to serve a whole new set of customers with entirely different set of needs. Hyperbole? Perhaps. And maybe, just maybe, it's a sign of things to come. I mention this because if you're not doing what you're passionate about in this new millennium then you are going to be chewed up and spit out. In this new paradigm, old dogs are going to have to learn new tricks or they're going to be on the outside looking in. Get with it. Figure out what you're passionate about and engage yourself . . . Well, what are you waiting for?

2 Jennifer Grant Haworth and Clifton Conrad, *Emblems of Quality in Higher Education* (Boston: Allyn and Bacon, 1997) 81-82

4
Life's More Like a Bobsled Run or a Bull-Run Than a Rollercoaster Ride.

"Life is difficult. This is a great truth, one of the greatest truths. It is a great truth because once we truly see this truth, we transcend it. Once we truly know that life is difficult—once we truly understand and accept it—then life is no longer difficult."
— M. Scott Peck, *The Road Less Traveled*

From the time we pop out of our mother's womb until they lower us into the ground, life is a continuous string of ups and downs, peaks and valleys, dips and curves, bends and bumps. All of us, whether we want to or not, are riding this thing called life and we're all headed somewhere. Some of us are moving along calmly, taking in the scenery, enjoying the journey. Some of us are moving at a frantic pace, running over anything or anybody in our way as if life were a race against the clock, while others of us are out of control, just holding on for dear life!

Along this life-ride, there will be satisfying highs that take our breaths away and disappointing lows that can make us feel like giving up and throwing in the towel. One moment we may find ourselves traveling through dark tunnels where we can't see our hand in front of our faces, then moments later find ourselves bursting out into the bright sunlight. No doubt, life has its share of difficulty, challenge, and pain, but it also has its share of magnificence, joy, and wonder.

Often an analogous comparison is made between life and a rollercoaster ride. I used to buy that, but not any more. Not since I bobsledded. While life does mimic a rollercoaster ride in terms of ups and downs, the similarities end there. Though it may seem so on the surface, life is really *not* much like a rollercoaster ride at all. Think about it. A rollercoaster only gives the illusion of risk. It's only an illusion because roller coasters actually ride on safety rails. We may *feel* as if we are going to crash, but not really, because in the back of our minds we know, or at least assume, the rollercoaster is built to stay on the tracks. Routine inspections are made to ensure safety. It's because we feel safe that we hold our hands in the air, laugh and scream, and enjoy the ride without any serious fear. We're riding with the knowledge that when it's all said and done, we'll get dropped off safe and sound and none the worse for wear. A rollercoaster ride gives a thrill without risk. Does that sound real world to you? All thrill, no risk, and no need for personal responsibility anywhere along the way other than following a few simple rules. For those who like roller-coasters, they're a bargain well worth the wait in line.

Tragically though, this is the same type mentality that many in our culture have fallen into. We want a life that guarantees our safety if we follow certain rules. We want security and to be taken care of. And we don't just want it, we demand it. We think it's our right to be happy! Even the U.S. Constitution doesn't guarantee us happiness, only the *pursuit* of it. The simple truth is; life comes with no guarantees. There are no safety rails to run on, no nets to catch us when we fall, and no one else is responsible for us, even if the perception of security is there.

Take our present economy for example. Most everyone assumed their money and jobs were safe. Nothing *could* happen or *would* happen. There were safety rails in place. Surely, the big wigs and the experts knew what they were doing. We could trust them. They were looking out for us. Yet, as millions have found out, it was all an illusion. There were no safety rails.

Instead of a rollercoaster ride, a more accurate analogy of life would be a bobsled run. In bobsledding, while there is a track, there are no security rails. (Okay, there are lips on the track to confine the carnage, but you get my point). You take on all the responsibility and all the risk. You train and prepare. You maintain your equipment and sled. You take all the needed precautions then give it your best shot and then hope for the best. That's as good as it gets. There simply aren't any guarantees. Anything can happen. Teammates can let you down or get injured. You could lose your footing on the ice or pull a hamstring. Accidents happen. People get hurt. Sometimes, although rarely, people even die.

So, what does life being like a bobsled run have to do with passion and courage? It has everything to do with it. I believe that most of us would readily agree with Mr. Scott Peck's assessment at the beginning of this chapter that life *is* difficult. We all from time to time trudge through the unforeseen and turbulent winds of adversity. Sometimes, even when we are doing the best we can, in a matter of seconds, we can find ourselves in the midst of brutal struggles that leave us feeling as if life were beating up on us. Accidents occur. Loved ones get sick. We get sick. We get laid off. People do things that hurt us. We make mistakes. Stock markets tumble. No matter how much we plan, or prepare, or use prevention, adversity still finds a way to surprise us. Struggle and adversity are as much a part of the human experience as sunrise and sunset. I'm not trying to be fatalistic, just realistic. Willie Jolley confirmed these sentiments in his wonderful book *A Setback Is a Setup for a Comeback:*

> Thomas Paine said, "*These are the times that try men's souls!*"_Yes, these are the times that try men's souls. These are also the times that try women's souls, and

children's souls, and senior citizen's souls. These are simply trying times. So were the days before you were born and so will be the days after you die. In other words, LIFE IS TRYING! Your parents had some trying times and your grandparents had some trying times and your great grandparents had trying times. And you are going to have trying times. . . . Let's make sure this point is clear: life is challenging. It was challenging yesterday, it is challenging today, and it will be challenging tomorrow.[3]

The truth is, we can have a great work ethic, do all the right things, make the smart choices, shoot for the stars, and still wind up crashing on the rocks because of things totally out of our control. One minute we can be on top of the world and the next minute at rock bottom, especially in today's volatile economy.

My home-based business has been on the decline for a couple of years now. Big clients are now small clients or are gone all together. Clients are cutting corners, which often leaves me out in the cold. Throw in the fact that I'm the sole breadwinner, and yeah, it's a little unnerving. And I'm not anticipating any bailout money from the government. So, it's up to me and me alone. When we embrace that cold reality, really take it to heart, it has a way of keeping us well-motivated. It sharpens the mind, pencils too. Focus is

---

3 Willie Jolley, *A Setback Is a Setup for a Comeback* (New York: St. Martins, 1999), 45.

easier to muster and maintain. We can't afford to play the victim. We have to do "whatever" it takes to put ourselves in a position to succeed. Otherwise, unlike in the movie Apollo 13, failure IS an option, Houston.

Those who find true success in life understand that adversity is a realistic part of it and embrace it. By embrace, I don't mean they look forward to or enjoy difficulty. I simply mean they understand that life is often unfair, unjust, and painful, and while they may be a *victim* of circumstance, they've chosen not to take on a *victim mentality*. They refuse to let their particular situation define who they are. Harvey S. Firestone said, *"Never allow yourself to be made a victim. Accept no one's definition of your life, but define yourself."*

This is what truly successful people do. While they do experience the struggle that goes along with adversity, instead of playing the victim card, they actually look for opportunity in their misfortune. Everything is an adventure. And that attitude, my friends, takes courage, lots of it. Nelson Mandela said, *"When individuals rise above their circumstances and use problems to push them to become more, they grasp greatness."*

In order to rise above our circumstances and let our problems push us to greatness, it is critical that we toss the victim mentality. In fact, getting rid of the victim mentality is foundational to everything in the rest of this book. It's impossible to live passionately, to face our fears, or dream out loud while still holding on to a victim mentality. Having a victim mentality is the one thing in life that *does* come with a guarantee. It guarantees that we will *never* overcome our circumstances, that we will *never* find lasting happiness and contentment, that we will *never* reach our potential, that our spirits *will* shrivel up and eventually die, and that we will *never* "grasp greatness." Having a victim mentality is the death knell to successful living.

Taking personal responsibility for my own situation has helped me operationalize a "whatever it takes" attitude. I've had to be flexible. This past Christmas shopping season I took on a side job with a popular package delivery company. My business is typically slow in December, so rather than thinking manual labor was beneath me, I jumped in and out of a truck all day long, ringing doorbells and dropping off packages. I admit to praying that I wouldn't ring a doorbell and see one of my clients answer the door.

It was this same attitude that led me to become a certified personal trainer. After over twelve years of working out of my home I found my business had a certain rhythm to it. I'd be busy for a few weeks, then quiet for a few weeks, and then back to busy again. To fill the slow periods, and to get out of the house and grab a little company, I decided to become a certified personal trainer. I had a passion for working out. I liked helping people that were also passionate about staying or getting in shape, so I bought the books and took the test.

Over the past few years, the rhythm to my business that I referred to above began to slow to the point of no discernible rhythm at all. I could take care of my family mind you, but unpredictably. This up and down state led me to re-join the advertising agency world after a twenty-some-year hiatus. A culture shock for sure, but hey, life is supposed to be an adventure, right?

Struggle and adversity are part of the human experience. Our prosperity has helped insulate us from that reality. I fell into that trap, too, so I'm not throwing any stones. My point is that reminders of life's uncertainty are not all bad. Absorbed with a healthy perspective, those reminders can lead to opportunity. Tom Asacker spoke this in his *Nine Predictions for 2009* when he said, *"The reality of the coming year is that the precipitous decline in the economy will create a collective pause; a 'space' of epic proportions for organizations and individuals. Yes, it will be unpleasant for many. But it will also be an opportunity in disguise for those willing to seize the moment."*

My 2007 version of accepting personal responsibility for my life came in the form of running with the bulls in Pamplona, Spain. If you're not familiar with it, it's a week long festival held every July. Each morning they release bulls weighing from twelve to thirteen hundred pounds over narrow, wet, cobblestone streets strewn full of people dressed in white pants and tops and with red bandannas wrapped around their necks. It's a centuries old tradition. It's pretty much open to anyone. However, once you slip under the barricades and onto the course, you are on your own. There are no waivers to sign, no paperwork spelling out the obvious—that you can get hurt, or even killed running with these animals. Similar to my bobsled experience, the condors came back to nest. They had to be shooed away and I had to grab fear by the horns. But in doing so I again never felt more alive.

Can you imagine running this race in the United States? I can't. If it were held here you'd probably have to attend a weekend class and spend hours signing your life away. And after weaving your way past the protesters, you'd probably find yourself under the gaze of personal injury lawyers stacked two or three deep behind the barricades. Each one prepared to argue negligence on the part of the event organizers, and equally prepared, of course, to absolve you of any and all personal responsibility in the whole affair.

No, life isn't like a rollercoaster ride. It's more like a bobsled run or a bull-run. There are no guarantees, but armed with passion, courage and a strong sense of personal responsibility, life can become an adventure and not a gauntlet. It's a choice. Viktor Frankl said about this, *"Between stimulus and response there is a space. In that space is our power to choose our response. In our response lies our growth and our freedom."* Throw away the victim mentality and make the passionate, courageous, choice.

5
Just Execute, Baby

"Even if you're on the right track, you'll
get run over if you just sit there."
— Will Rogers

In the field of Physics; Einstein, Newton, Galileo,
Aristotle, and other scientific giants showed us that we
live in a universe based on movement. It was Albert Einstein
who said, *"Nothing happens until something moves."*

Aristotle said, *"We must take for granted that the things
that exist by nature are in motion."* Paul Henri Thiry added,
*"The universe, that vast assemblage of every thing that exists,
presents only matter and motion . . . an uninterrupted
succession of causes and effects."*

Motion is what keeps the universe growing, evolving,
changing, and from literally flying apart. Everything in the
universe, from an idea to a solid rock, from the smallest
electron to the largest galaxy, is in a perpetual state of

motion. Even when we appear *not* to be moving, we're in motion. At some specific point in history, at the beginning of time as we know it, energy and light exploded in a Big Bang, pushing the elements outward into a continuous flow of motion. Along this path of movement, that we've come to understand as time, some pretty awesome things have occurred—stars, planets, galaxies, black holes, water, air, atmosphere, dirt, atoms, molecules, amoebas, D.N.A., sparrows and eagles, minnows and whales, bacteria, butterflies, and blondes! The universe is all about motion and when the motion stops, life stops.

Motion is at work in our physical bodies as well. When we cease to move or exert energy for prolonged periods of time, the Law of Atrophy kicks in and our muscles begin to reverse. They shrivel up and deteriorate. In fact, this Law of Atrophy applies to nearly everything. When things are inactive they move towards decrease not increase, decay not development. Just park a brand new car then don't touch it for a few years and see what happens. To keep the car up it must be started, driven, and serviced on a regular basis otherwise it automatically goes into disrepair. In reality there is no such thing as neutral. Inaction never equals neutrality. Whether we feel it or not, something is always occurring. We're either moving forward and growing or moving backwards and decaying. It's one or the other, but something *is* always occurring.

While these fixed universal laws of physics are proven scientific facts, I believe they apply to other realms of our lives as well. In our relationships, careers, and life in general, we are either moving forwards or backwards, growing or decaying. There is no neutral. All the principles we've talked about up until this point that deal with growing courage and living passionately mean absolutely nothing without execution. It is one thing to uncover our inner passion, but it's a whole different thing to implement that passion into our daily lives. And when we are not implementing, we are not in a neutral state. We *are* going backwards.

Execution is all about getting our lives into forward, positive motion. Yet, it's much more than just taking action. It's about dealing with our fears, some of which are based on nothing more than not wanting to deviate from the comfort of the status quo. It's about taking that first, all important, step and then staying in motion, keeping up, and building momentum as you go.

Four Elements of Successful Execution

1) Dealing With Fear

A vital element in successful execution is dealing with your fears. I know that's easier said than done. To lead a full life, however, that's what has to happen. Fear confines us to comfort zones. Fear keeps us from seizing opportunities, tears down our vitality, encourages compromise, and hinders us from developing deeper relationships. It's virtually impossible to live an authentic, passionate, life when ruled by fear. Henry David Thoreau said, *"Nothing is so much to be feared as fear."* And who amongst us hasn't heard the immortal words that FDR uttered during his first inaugural address, *"The only thing we have to fear is fear itself."* Yes, fear is a real and present negative force.

On the flip side, however, fear can be a positive, motivating force. Fear can stop us dead in our tracks, but it can also nudge us into action. Basically, there are two types of fear, healthy and unhealthy. One leads to the preservation of life, the other to the destruction of life. To execute successfully it is imperative that we be able to discern the difference between the two.

Healthy fear is an essential tool fashioned for our protection. An absence of it would create a deficiency in our personality causing a shortage of common sense. Healthy fear keeps us from doing hazardous and foolish things. It's an internal warning system indicating that danger is near—a self-correcting mechanism hardwired into our brains meant to be uncomfortable enough to motivate us to action and distance ourselves from the threat.

Back in my twenties, before my bobsledding days, I worked as a bouncer in New York even though I only weighed about 190 pounds. That's pretty small for a bouncer and let me tell you, I learned a few lessons in healthy fear. One time, this crazy guy hopped up on top of the bar naked as a jaybird and started dancing. I was thinking, *"I'm pretty sure we don't have a license for this. He's gotta go."* I started walking towards the bar and someone yelled out, *"You don't want to take him off the bar. You take that boy off the bar and you'll have this whole bar on your ass!"* The person who said this to me didn't say it with any hostility in his voice, he was just telling me like it was. My response was pretty practical. *"OK, he can stay."* Another time, I ended up squaring off with three or four guys and my *"self-correcting mechanism"* kicked in. I hit the exit door in an all out sprint with the four dudes in hot pursuit. All four of them would have beaten the hell out of me, but they'd have to catch me first and that wasn't going to happen. That's healthy fear!

Recently, there was a report on the news about a nineteen year old boy and two of his friends who had lost their lives in a tragic automobile accident. He was driving his car so fast that he lost control and hit a tree head on. The police confirmed the vehicle had been traveling in access of one hundred miles per hour. Most of the people who knew this young man also knew he had an attitude. One of his girlfriends being interviewed said that she'd ridden with him at speeds of over a hundred miles an hour. He was hot. He was arrogant. He had a sticker on his car that read in big, bold letters *"NO FEAR."* He's now dead. His epitaph could read, *"NO FEAR, NO RESPECT, NOW DEAD."* It's a tragic story. He could have used a dose of healthy fear.

Healthy fear not only protects us from danger but it motivates us to get moving into action. Animals in the wild know instinctively that if they don't keep moving they'll be eaten alive. Likewise, fear that keeps us moving and the adrenaline pumping, can be a good thing.

Unhealthy fear however, is a dangerous fear that controls, overwhelms, consumes, and paralyzes us. To compensate for it we lock ourselves in our comfort zones that give us the allusion of safety but, in reality, are self-made prisons that rob us of our ultimate potential and leave us discontented. It's this kind of fear that we must overcome if we are going to live with authenticity and passion. Growth and success always contain a certain amount of risk and risk always contains some level of fear.

The different types of unhealthy fears that hold us hostage are numerous and varied. However, the majority of them stem from one basic root fear—the fear of failure. The reason most people don't step out and take a leap of faith is because of the fear of failure. *"What if the relationship doesn't work out and I'm hurt . . . again?" "What if my product doesn't sell?" "What if people think I'm crazy?" "What if I'm rejected?"* What if? What if? What if? And these *"what ifs?,"* even though they may appear to be very legitimate, are almost always bigger in our minds than in reality.

But having said that, the bottom line is this; if you are going to reach your potential in life and live your passion, you are going to have to overcome your fear of failure. The truth of the matter is; most highly successful people in the world are people who know failure quite well and are not afraid of it. Instead of fearing it, they often embrace it. They've realized that it's okay to fail PROVIDED that they learn from their mistakes. Everything else they kick to the curb. They don't burden themselves with unnecessary baggage. They've learned the secrets of *failing often* and *failing forward.* That is, they use failure as a stepping stone to success. Charles C. Manz, Ph.D., is a professor of Business Leadership at the University of Massachusetts and has served as a consultant for numerous Fortune 500 companies. Dr. Manz wrote a book entitled, *The Power of Failure.* Just that title alone speaks volumes. There can be a tremendous power in failure. He said, *"If you want to be more successful, double your failure rate and recognize failure as the lifeblood of success."* Wow, those are some pretty heavy statements. "Double your failure rate to be more successful? Failure is the lifeblood of success?" He continues, *"If someone never fails, this is a telltale sign that he is not trying anything new or challenging. Mastering new skills and growing as individuals require that we enter unfamiliar arenas that can provide us with new knowledge and capabilities."*[4]

I believe Dr. Manz is right on. One thing is for certain, if you do not overcome your fear of failure it will absolutely shut you down. But if you can harness the fear of it, failure can actually work for you. Consider the story of successful author and speaker Barry Farber who also learned to fail forward.

My first book, *Breakthrough Selling,* was turned down by twenty-six publishers before one finally

---

4 Charles C. Manz, *The Power of Failure* (San Francisco: BK, 2002) 13 – 21.

bought it. Talk about rejection! Now I know why so many talented writers don't get their work published. When they're constantly exposed to that type of rejection, their confidence and their perseverance get worn down. Sure, after the first rejection I was disturbed, but not devastated. Five or six rejections later, however, I was starting to get very concerned.

Then I called my agent and asked what the problem was. He said that there were just so many other books out there on sales that publishers were hesitant to take on another one. But I knew I had a fresh approach and important ideas to add to an admittedly crowded field. So after the next rejection, I called the publisher and asked what I could do to improve my chances. What was missing from my book? What did it need to make it stand our and invite acceptance?

I followed the next rejection with a similar phone call, and the next and the next. Suggested changes were made. Now I looked forward to each rejection. Without even knowing it, these publishers were helping me write my book!

The valuable lesson I learned was not to equate rejection with failure. When the twenty-seventh publisher bought my book, he was not getting a manuscript that had failed twenty-six times. He was getting a manuscript that had benefited from the advice of twenty-six talented, knowledgeable professionals.

Of course, I'm not the only writer who's ever had to deal with rejection. Robert Shook was an insurance agent for seventeen years before he became an author. His first book was rejected twenty-two times. But he believed in the work and didn't give up on it. Thirty-six books later, Shook has interviewed and written about some of the most successful people in our country, and has come to some conclusions about their success. "Successful people are able to accept failure and not be defeated by it," he says. "They go from failure to failure and still not fail."[5]

I made failure work for me in my bobsled experience. My first attempt ended in utter failure. I was disappointed and embarrassed with my performance. However, with the passage of a few days came some objectivity—I hadn't prepared myself properly and got what I deserved. In that moment of brutal honesty with myself I realized that if I was to have any chance at making the team then I'd have to try again, but this time well-prepared and respectful of the sport that I was trying to gain entry into. Soon, my disappointment and embarrassment was replaced by the knowledge that came from my past mistakes and

---

5 Barry Farber, *Diamonds In The Rough, The Secret to Finding Your Own Value—and Making Your Own Success* (New York: Berkley, 1995), 56.

determination. I was then on my way to making the team. I had truly failed forward.

To fail forward successfully you have to develop the skill of positioning your failures to yourself in an honest and constructive manner. A good example is when I learned I had literally been conned out of $25,000 by two "supposed" business partners. I was devastated by the loss, and particularly the way it occurred. Yet, I quickly rebounded after talking with a close friend who confessed that he too had lost money in a legitimate business investment. He said to me, *"Jim, what does it matter how we lost our money, either way it's gone."* He was right. He positioned my loss honestly, but constructively, and because of that I was able to learn from what happened and moved on much wiser. Did it hurt? You bet. But it was a learning experience that made me stronger.

How we position fear and failure in our minds is critical. Madison Avenue spends billions of dollars positioning things, and they're good at it, too. It would serve us well to take a few notes from them. They work hard at positioning their products to give them the best opportunity to succeed but ultimately know that they can't guarantee success. That's up to the buyers.

During the Korean War, Army and Marine forces found themselves over-extended and under constant threat from the enemy. They had to head back to the coast to escape. The Press, which was following the developments, referred to it as a 'retreat.' When confronted with that interpretation, Marine Corps Major General O.P. Smith said, *"Retreat? Hell, we're attacking in a different direction."* That was the ultimate in positioning—brutally honest, yet constructive and positive at the same time. Calling it a retreat might have turned the trip to the coast into a track meet. By using the word 'attacking', he changed the entire mindset of those involved. How you position your fear and failure in your mind is critical. Be honest with yourself, but be constructive.

Everything I have just said probably rings true to you on an intellectual level. You know fear can be paralyzing. You know fear has to be overcome. You know failure is a part of life and that you need to persevere. You know you need to learn from your mistakes and that you need to stay positive. But being armed with this intellectual understanding does not necessarily translate into walking the walk, does it? Something is missing. A very common misconception with regard to fear is that it needs to be stared down, beaten down, and tossed to the side like a piece of garbage. Horse hockey! It doesn't work that way. When I tried out for the bobsled team I had a terrible little secret—I was, and still am, afraid of roller coasters. Stand up to that fear, hell no! I still hate roller coasters and avoid them at all costs to this day. The trick for me in overcoming this fear wasn't standing up to it, it was seeing through it to what was on the other side. And what was on the other side was something I was passionate about—i.e. getting an opportunity to make it to the Olympic Games. The reason why I hate roller coasters so much is there is nothing waiting for me on the other side except fear. I don't like being scared to death and getting nauseated just for kicks! There needs to be a reason behind it. If we find ourselves consumed by fear what we are really saying is that there is little in front of us. Goals that we are passionate about pull us past and through our fears. And let there be no doubt, if we are not passionate about a goal, fear will gladly fill the vacuum.

2) Pushing Off

The second element necessary for successful execution is actually pushing off. My role on the four-man bobsled team was that of a sprinter. In bobsledding, the push is absolutely critical because man-power and gravity are the only two forces in the contest. At first glance it may seem like a rather simple process; just find a couple of really strong, fast, guys and get the sled moving down the track as fast as possible. But when hundredths of a second are the difference between winning and losing, Gold and Silver, staying and going home, things can get a bit more complicated. Actually, there is a science to the push. In fact, the U.S. Bobsled Federation is now conducting studies and running tests with MIT aerodynamic engineers on how to maximize the push along with other important elements of the sport. The general rule of thumb is that for every tenth of a second shaved off the push time, three-tenths of a second can be subtracted at the finish line.

But here's the deal. My teammates and I could practice, prepare, watch films, participate in scientific studies, talk and plan about what we were going to do, yet, our sled would do absolutely nothing but sit on the track until our planning was put into action. We had to actually grab the handles, get into the launching position, dig our spikes into the ice, and then in unison, explode into motion. Getting a good push off is critical to successful execution. I know it sounds so incredibly simple and commonsensical. However, my question is this: If taking action is so simple, then how come so many people make great plans, have deep seated dreams and passions, but they never do anything about them? They're like a bobsled just sitting on the track and as Will Rogers said, "... you'll get run over if you just sit there."

Admittedly, taking that very first step of action is the toughest. But again, it is a choice. In his book *Monday Morning Choices*, David Cottrell says:

Making choices is a privilege, one that gives us a freedom we should never take for granted. A graduate researcher, after a week of following an inmate's schedule from dawn to dusk each day at a state penitentiary, reported that the most difficult part of prison life was its lack of choices. "Inmates are denied choices over when life happens, from when to arise each day to when to shower, exercise, work, eat, or retire," she said. "It was one of the most traumatic experiences of my life."

Isn't it interesting? In our free and democratic society, punishment comes in the form of reducing people's ability to make even the most basic choices in their everyday lives. Those inmates will confirm that life without choices is no way to live. Our choices are our privilege! Life is filled with pressures that force us to make constant and immediate choices. Yet, as the prison researcher found, a life without choices is not a good way to live.

Think it's too late to embrace a new philosophy? Or maybe you're worried that you can't make the right choices? It is never too late! According to psychologist Abraham Maslow, "The story of the human race is the story of men and women selling themselves short." Don't sell yourself short. You can make better choices beginning today to achieve what you want in life tomorrow.[6]

Face it, there are a lot of things that we want to experience in life, but few of us are willing to actually take the steps to turn them into reality, the first two steps being dealing with fear and then making the choice of getting into motion. We tend to have this *"I'm along for the ride"* mentality as if we have no real choice in the

---

6 David Cottrell, *Monday Morning Choices, 12 Powerful Ways to Go From Everyday to Extraordinary* (New York: HarperCollins, 2007), xvii.

matter. As a result, we let the ride of life take us where *it* would have us to go. Well, at some point, we must pull ourselves out of the back seat, grab a hold of the wheel, and take control.

Let's take this present economy for example. None of us have a crystal ball that will give us a clear vision of the future. If we did, we wouldn't be in this mess to start with. The best way to determine your future is to take charge of creating it. Take some personal responsibility. Grab the wheel and get moving! Roll up your sleeves, let your inner passion and what matters most to you be your roadmap, and get to work on your dreams. Robert Frost said so aptly, *"The reason worry kills more people than work, is that more people worry than work."*

When I had my own business people would often tell me, "It must really be nice to be your own boss." That comment always made me laugh because I had bosses, too. They were called clients. The point is; everybody works for somebody and everyone works for themselves. Even if you're working for someone else's company, you're still responsible for your own choices. We are all on our own. To think otherwise is a delusion.

When we recognize our ability to make choices, then difficulties, like the economy, can offer many great opportunities for those individuals who are alert, who are willing to be flexible and take calculated risks, and are not afraid to work. Thomas A. Edison said, *"We often miss opportunity because it's dressed in overalls and looks like work."*

Even when we hit bottom, and I've been there, we still have a choice. We can hit bottom and stay there, or we can use the bottom to push off of and struggle back to the surface. Remember this; whenever we are frustrated or confronted with a deep dilemma, there's usually a hidden opportunity waiting to be uncovered and acted on.

Sometimes it is necessary to manufacture the dramatic in order for real change to occur in our lives. When you look at those who've experienced an unusual degree of success, quite often they created it by attempting the dramatic. In other words, most people would have called them crazy or pursuing a pipe dream. Never mind what others said, they were driven by their passion and refused to be dissuaded by the naysayers.

Henry Ford was past middle age when the idea of the Model T car came to him. His friends thought it was a crazy idea and he had great difficulty raising capital. *"A horseless carriage, what's that?"* people would ask. *"Who'd ever want one of those?"* His father tearfully said to him once, *"Henry, why do you give up a good twenty-five dollar a week job in order to chase this crazy idea?"* Despite his critics, Henry Ford created the dramatic and acted on it. It changed his life and the world would never be the same for it.

When Walt Disney came up with the idea of building a theme park based on a cartoon mouse with big ears, the number of people who thought he was nuts was too high to count. Financial institutes simply laughed at the concept of Disneyland and wouldn't give him a dime for the project. Undeterred, Walt took a risk and borrowed money from his personal life insurance policy so he could take a step of action. I'd say that's pretty dramatic. And where would the world be without Disney?

Pushing off is about making a choice—sometimes a dramatic choice—and then acting on it. Of course, we must be careful to make sound choices based on knowing ourselves and our situations. By sound choices I mean decisions that are based on knowing who we are and what moves us. One thing is for certain, if we do not start moving towards whatever we want in life, we are absolutely 100% assured of not to getting it. By not taking action we are sealing our destiny before we've even began.

If your goals seem too overwhelming, start small, with baby steps. "*The journey of a thousand miles begins with a single step,*" said Lao Tzu. Gandhi recognized the importance of taking action when he said, "*You may never know what result comes from your action, but if you do nothing there will be no result.*" Olympic Gold medalist Bruce Jenner put it in a more practical way. He said, "*Sometimes, you've got to get up in the morning, look life square in the face, and get on with it.*" The second element of successful execution is pushing off into action.

3) Breaking Out
The third element necessary for successful execution is breaking out—breaking out and freeing ourselves from

our personal comfort zones. And while there is certainly nothing wrong with living a life of comfort and having our daily needs met, being controlled by comfort is the death knell to courageous, passionate living. In fact, it can be downright lethal to healthy living. T. Harv Ecker author of *Secrets of the Millionaire Mind*, boldly proclaimed, *"Nobody ever died of discomfort, yet in the name of comfort has killed more ideas, more opportunities, more actions, and more growth than everything else combined. Comfort kills!"*

Researchers at the University of California Berkeley did an experiment in which they placed an amoeba into a completely comfortable, safe, and stress-free environment—idyllic temperature, perfect blend of moisture, and a constant food supply. Everything necessary for health and comfort was provided. Guess what happened? The amoeba died. The researchers discovered that they had given the amoeba everything it needed, except a struggle. What the amoeba required, in addition to food, was a challenge to survive![7] Too much comfort really does kill. The great abolitionist Frederick Douglas put it this way, "Where there is no struggle, there is no progress."

Wikipedia gives one of the best definitions of the comfort zone. It says, *"One's comfort zone refers to the set of environments and behaviors with which one is comfortable, without creating a sense of risk. A comfort*

---

7 John Ortberg, *If You Want To Walk On Water, You've Got To Get Out Of The Boat* (Grand Rapids, Michigan: Zondervan, 2001) 47.

zone is a type of mental conditioning that causes a person to create and operate mental boundaries that are not real. <u>Such boundaries create an unfounded sense of security</u>. *Like inertia, a person who has established a comfort zone in a particular axis of his or her life, will tend to stay within that zone without stepping outside of it.* <u>Highly successful persons may routinely step outside their comfort zones to accomplish what they wish.</u> "[8]

I love that last sentence. "Highly successful persons may routinely step outside their comfort zones to accomplish what they wish." Likewise, highly unsuccessful people routinely shrink back inside the perceived safety of their comfort zones to accomplish dissatisfaction, complacency, predictability, boredom, and everything that is opposite of courage and passion.

The problem with the comfort zone is its too comfortable! For those living in their comfort zones, life isn't brilliant and fulfilling, but it's not uncomfortable enough to do anything about it. So, instead of taking action, they simply go along with the flow of other's expectations and where life is taking them, never finding the courage to break free and follow their true passions. Because of this, sometimes being knocked out of our comfort zone by outside forces can most definitely be a blessing in disguise. It forces us to make needed changes. Though they may be uncomfortable, and even painful at the time, things like getting laid off, going through

8 Quoted from http://en.wikipedia.org/wiki/Comfort_zone

an unwanted divorce, or other adverse circumstances, could be the best thing that ever happened to a person! A disappointment could actually be a stepping stone towards a more fulfilling reappointment.

People who give too much authority to their comfort zones never experience greatness. Instead, their lives resemble broken elephants. In Asia, it's not uncommon to see massive four or five ton elephants being held to trees by small, single, ropes tied to their front legs. With no chains attached, the elephants could easily break free at anytime, but they don't. You see, when the elephants are very young their trainers use the same size rope to tie them to trees. The baby elephants pull, yank, and struggle to break free but at that age the rope is strong enough to hold them. As they grow, they are conditioned to believe they cannot break away. By the time they are full grown, even though they could break free, they believe they can't so they don't even try.

Eventually, because of their limiting belief system, and because their bellies are always full, the elephants become quite comfortable in their restricted lifestyle. In the rare cases that an elephant does break free it's usually the result of some kind of outside trauma that forces the animal to impulsively break out.

Just like the baby elephants, most of us have been conditioned to believe certain limiting and false ideas about ourselves. As a result, we lean towards and become accustomed to the safe and familiar. The great danger of the comfort zone is that we slowly become lulled into a life of inaction. And remember, there is no such thing as neutral because by nature things are either growing or decaying. If we don't force ourselves at times to break out of our comfort zones, we will settle for the life of a broken elephant and eventually, just like our amoeba friend, our passion for life will die.

In contrast to the broken elephant, consider for a moment the lives of the wild gazelle and lion in Africa. The following paints a tremendous picture.

> *Every morning in Africa, a gazelle wakes up. It knows that it must run faster than the fastest lion or it will be killed. Every morning in Africa, a lion wakes up. It knows that it must run faster than the slowest gazelle or it will starve. It doesn't matter whether you're a lion or a gazelle; when the sun comes up, you had better start running.*[9]

I like that. Living a life of courageous passion, outside our comfort zone, is like waking up every morning on the run. It's a life of personal responsibility, not dependability. It's a life where you learn to trust in your own instincts, abilities, gifts, and eventually discover that there's more security in them than inside your comfort zone. Sure, it's sometimes scary, but it's the only way to live and the only way to fulfillment.

---

9 Robert Ringer, *Action! Nothing Happens Until Something Moves* (New York: M. Evans and Company, 2004), 16.

4) Keep Moving

Now that you've gotten into motion by dealing with your fears, pushing off into action, and breaking out of your comfort zones, it's imperative to keep moving and not let anything stop you. You see, by being in motion, not only are you heading in the direction of your goal, but along the way you are allowing yourself to be in positions for significant opportunities that could not happen if you were not moving. In addition, being in motion causes another dynamic to occur, the dynamic of momentum.

At the start of a bobsled race, when my team began pushing off our sled, it took maximum effort for us to get the 1,500 pound piece of equipment launched, but once it was in motion, the sled required less and less of our energy to keep it going. As it picked up speed the sled started gaining momentum and eventually became like a missile shooting down the track at eighty to ninety miles per hour with concentrated force and power. By then, the energy necessary from the team had switched from pushing to guiding. Basically, we were along for the ride simply making sure we stayed on course for the finish line.

Sir Isaac Newton's Law of Motion was never more a factor than when bobsledding. And, as I stated earlier in the chapter, I believe these laws of physics can be a powerful analogy for our everyday lives and that holds true when talking about momentum as well. Best selling author and speaker Brian Tracy explains it well in his book *Create Your Own Future.* He says:

> One of the most important luck factors of all is called the Momentum Strategy for Success. It is based on the principle of inertia. This principle, paraphrased from Sir Isaac Newton, says, 'A person in motion tends to remain in motion; it takes much less energy to keep moving than it does to stop and try to start moving again.'
>
> For example, you may require ten units of energy to get yourself moving initially, but then you only need one or two units of energy to keep moving. However, if you stop for any reason, it can take you another ten units of energy to get yourself going once more. This is why many people who stop never get going again. This principle explains why it is that successful people are moving targets. They are always in motion. Keep yourself in continuous motion. Get going and then keep going.[10]

Most of the time, it's difficult to get moving in a new direction in life. The more we're locked into our comfort zones, the deeper we sink into our ruts, and the more inertia it takes to get out. However, once we are out of the rut and are moving in the direction we want to go, by staying consistent, we, little by little, start picking

---

10 Brian Tracy, *Create Your Own Future* (New York: Wiley & Sons, Inc., 2002), 197

up speed, and eventually the momentum takes over. It's when we enter the momentum phase of life that we begin seeing real progress and results. According to Jack Canfield, "Momentum is that [magical] unseen energy force that brings more opportunity, more resources, and more people who can help you into your life at seemingly just the right time."[11] Quitting before we reach the momentum phase can often be a huge mistake.

Momentum is going our way in life when we've taken the arduous steps to move in a particular direction and then, at some point along the journey, things become balanced and we find yourself going with the flow. We are now guiding instead of pushing. It's kind of like a surfer who has paddled way out from shore in search of the perfect wave and now has found it and is riding it in.

When we've recognized a wave of momentum we want to ride it as long as we can, letting the force of it carry us forward. The key at this point is to maintain our balance and stay the course. When we sense the onset of negative inertia pulling us under, we need to resist it and fight back. We can't be surprised at problems. Understand that complications, mistakes, snags, and delays are inevitable. Expect them. No matter how well we plan or how hard we work, things can always change and require us to react. Be ready for them but always keep moving forward. Remember, when we stop, the momentum dies and we sink.

---

11 Jack Canfield, *The Success Principles* (New York: HarperCollins, 205), 109.

One of the foremost ways, if not *the* foremost way we allow negative inertia to slow us down or completely stop our momentum is by having unrealistic expectations. That is, instead of expecting difficulty we expect smooth rides with no problems or needed adjustments along the way and for our plans to unfold exactly like we've projected. In addition to unrealistic expectations, we often become victims of what I call the *analysis paralysis syndrome.* That's when we get so caught up in the details of our plans that when things call for *"on the spot"* flexibility and ingenuity we get bogged down or stuck.

A lawyer friend of mine once told me that his particular department was known as the Sales Prevention Department. Why? Because they are paid to look at the world in terms of what COULD happen negatively. A lawyer's education and training is basically contrary to a real understanding of what it takes to succeed. It's a legal mentality rooted in paranoia and exaggerated fear of what COULD happen. This mentality keeps people tied down like the fictional character, Gulliver. Please know that I'm in no way trying to bash attorneys. A good one sure does come in handy when you're in trouble. The problem is, when we lead our lives based on that mentality it slams the brakes on our momentum and many good opportunities get killed in the vetting process.

Now hear me on this. Preparation is vital. We must always be well prepared and do our homework. It's foolish to move forward without counting the cost and taking the necessary precautions to protect ourselves. I wouldn't think of doing a bobsled run without a helmet. Being unprepared and unprotected is a sure-fire way to fail. Yet, there will never be a point when everything is perfect. That's living in Narcissismville. To live a life of courageous passion we've got to get moving and keep moving, even when things aren't perfect. The important thing is to get underway and then make adjustments as we go.

Writing a book is another great analogy for what I'm talking about. E.L. Doctorow said, *"Planning to write is not writing."* The truth is; writing a book is really more about editing. Bestselling author James Michener said, "I'm not a very good writer, but I'm an excellent rewriter!" Isaac Bashevis Singer said, *"The wastebasket is a writer's best friend."* Why? It's because a book is almost always a work in motion. For most writers, the ones that I know anyway, they're never exactly sure where the book is ultimately going until well after they've begun the process of putting pen to paper or type to page. After that, the work unfolds in capricious and unpredictable ways. The point is; vision and planning are necessary to start, but the significant insights are more apt to come through doing and editing—from being in motion. Writing, like life, is more about the journey than the destination. The sooner we learn this, the better. Too much speculating and strategizing can slam the brakes on progress.

In 1962 President Kennedy gave his famous "Go to the Moon" speech. In it, he said, *"We choose to go to the moon. We choose to go to the moon in this decade and do the other things, not because they are easy, but because they are hard, because that goal will serve to organize and measure the best of our energies and skills, because that challenge is one that we are willing to accept, one we are unwilling to postpone, and one which we intend to win, and the others, too."* Kennedy didn't know how we were going to do it, nobody did, but in July, 1969, that's exactly what we did. Sometimes you just have to jump in and take on the challenges as they present themselves.

When I ran with the bulls I had a plan going in. I had developed a plan after watching videos of past races. I would start running when the people coming from further up the course started to run past me in numbers. While standing in the crowd waiting, I got another nugget of advice—to watch for flashes of cameras in the balconies. This would be my sign to start running. Great. I had two cues to go on. After the crowd spread out along the track, I assumed my position on the course. The final seconds ticked by and then I heard it, the first firework indicating the first bull has left the corral. Shortly thereafter, I heard the second firework alerting everyone that all the bulls were out of the corral and on the course. Now it was only a matter time.

The crowds that had gathered to run and to watch the drama unfold craned their necks to get a look at the bulls barreling down the street. I saw the flash bulbs going off. The bulls were close. But where are all the people I assumed would be streaming by? While I tried to sort this out, a strange smell filled my nostrils. It was the smell of bulls on my ass! "Wait a minute, this wasn't part of my plan," I thought. Yeah, well guess what? Several tons of muscle bound, pissed off, snot snorting bovines didn't give a hoot about my plan. I was in their way and would be dealt with accordingly. At that point, I saw through my fears (rather quickly I might add!) to my goal—living— not getting a horn up my . . . ! My courageous passion had become very practical. I was like the gazelle because my options were survive or else.

Apparently, at least on that particular section of the course, many of the runners didn't run, they *stood* and watched the bulls. (Note to self: Study more video next time.) What did I do? I improvised and started running as fast as I could. Running down the narrow street, I soon found out that the people lined up against the walls and in the doorways did not want to give up their spots. Some people, or so it seemed, took great joy in pushing runners back into the middle of the street. Eventually, I insisted on a spot along the wall with all the vigor that a two-hundred-twenty-pound fifty-year-old man running for his life could insist on. Whew, I made it! My point is this; some insights don't reveal themselves until we are engaged. We simply make adjustments and keep going. It's when we stop moving, that we're in trouble!

More often than not, life isn't like a carefully laid out business plan. Although we must certainly plan and use common sense, leaps of faith are still required. And some things you'll only be able to figure out once you are engaged. Much of the planning I did prior to my arrival in Pamplona went out the window once the race began. Added clarity comes from being under pressure. Priorities become clear. Options narrow. Decisiveness reigns supreme. But none of this can happen in our comfort zones. It takes boots on the ground. There's just no other way around it.

6
Keeping the Spirit
of Adventure Alive

*"Security is mostly a superstition. It does not exist in
nature. Life is either a grand adventure or nothing.*
— Helen Keller

Being able to do for a living what we're truly passionate
about isn't always possible. I mean, let's keep it real.
If I was living my passion 100% I'd probably be a bush
pilot somewhere. I can't do that now because I have kids
to finish rearing. What I can do, however, what we all
can do for that matter, is live passionately. There is a
difference. Living passionately is not about just tasting
life, but savoring every bite of it. It involves a heightening
of our senses and seeing life, both its highs and lows, as "a
grand adventure or nothing."

Whether it's bobsledding, or a part-time gig with a
package delivery service, it's all part of the adventure.

Tackling life with passion, as an adventure, is really not about succeeding or failing. It's about letting the kid in you see the adventure in everything you do. Think about it. When we were kids we were passionate about life because everything was fresh and alive. The ordinary was amazing. The common was sacred. We were absolutely enchanted with life—not money—not career—not prestige—but simply life. As kids we'd burst into the house with excitement oozing out of every pore. The words couldn't come out fast enough. The simplest of things captivated us. We could skip rocks along the water endlessly and never tire. We could run around with jars trying to capture lightening bugs like our life depended on it. We loved life, appreciated the simple, and were captivated by the familiar. But somewhere in the transition between childhood and adulthood we let the wonder slip away as we began to pursue more important, *"mature"* things. Well, we desperately need to recapture the wonder because it's the wonder that's going to sustain us. The more our vision for life becomes childlike, the more we will see the marvelous in the mundane, and the more adventurous our lives will become.

I like to compare life to a book with many different chapters. As each of us travel through our own particular book of life, some chapters will naturally come to a close as we enter new ones. How we handle these transitions has everything to do with the flow of our lives. Transitions mean change and change is something that we typically tend to resist rather than embrace. Instead of resisting change however, at the transitions in your life, learn to say goodbye to the old chapters by taking from them all you can and letting them grow you. Become stronger, wiser, and tender towards life, and then embrace the next chapter as a grand adventure. This is the way life is meant to be lived—experiencing it fully and wide-open. Webster defines passion as "intense emotion or driving force." When living passionately there's a driving force infusing our lives. It gives us energy, motivation, focus, and excitement. Pursuing life passionately as an adventure sustains us when some of those chapters are difficult.

For a moment, consider the life of Helen Keller who wrote the quote at the beginning of this chapter. As most of you probably know, she was both blind and deaf. Yet, despite her tremendous limitations, Helen Keller experienced success beyond that of most "normal" people. She was the first deaf/blind person to earn a Bachelor of Arts degree and went on to become a world-famous speaker and author. She's remembered as a political activist who campaigned for women's suffrage, workers' rights, as well as many other progressive causes. In 1915 she founded the Helen Keller International Organization which is devoted to research in vision, health, and nutrition. Keller traveled to over 39 countries and met every US President from Grover Cleveland to Lyndon B. Johnson. She was friends with many famous figures, including Alexander Graham Bell, Charlie Chaplin, and Mark Twain. Helen Keller accomplished all of that while being deaf and blind! I can't even comprehend that. My friend, whatever we are experiencing, we are without excuse.

The reason I elaborated on Helen Keller's success is because according to her, one of the ways she thrived in life instead of survived was by approaching the obstacles and new chapters in her life as *"grand"* adventures. Here is what she said about life's transitions, *"When one door closes another door opens; But we so often look so long and so regretfully upon the closed door, that we do not see the ones which open for us."* She also said, *"Everything has its wonders, even darkness and silence. . . One should never count the years—one should instead count one's interests. I have kept young trying never to lose my childhood sense of wonderment. . ."* There you have it. Even in the midst of her incredible challenges, Helen Keller never gave in to self-pity and she never lost the wonder or adventure of life.

My life has indeed been a series of many chapters. Some of those chapters, like the bobsledding adventure, had a powerful impact on the rest of my life. And now, after all the years, I presently find myself preparing to enter yet more chapters. I have a new career. I've sold the house that I have lived in for the past seventeen years and bought another. I'm putting the finishing touches on this book, and in time, will set out to begin a speaking career.

Ralph Waldo Emerson captured my sentiments perfectly in regards to taking chances in life. He wrote, *"All life is an experiment. The more experiments you make the better. What if they are a little course, and you may get your coat soiled? What if you do fail, and get fairly rolled in the dirt once or twice? Up again, you shall never be so afraid of a tumble."*

This ole' dog wants to learn new tricks even if it does mean taking a roll in the dirt every now and then. The way I see it, in this uncertain economy, that attitude adds up to versatility and opportunities. It's funny, but I've heard a lot of people telling me lately that it looks like they'll be working well past the age of sixty-five. They say it like it's a curse or something—like it's some sort of punishment that they are going to have to live through, but it could be the best thing that ever happened to them.

The whole idea of retiring at sixty-five is a fairly recent notion. In 1935, when the United States passed its first Social Security laws deeming 65 the legal retirement age, the average life expectancy in America was only 61.7 years. If we applied that same scale to today, the current retirement age should be around 81 years! As for me, I never want to retire. I may slow down a bit and change my focus, but retire? Hell no! People that retire from passionate living and adventure have already begun the dying process. Thanks but no thanks. I'll pass on that one.

Don't get me wrong. I get scared just like everybody else, especially with this present state of world affairs and the economy. But I'm learning to see through my fears to the things that I'm passionate about, and that gives me courage. When I do this I feel energized instead of overwhelmed, excited more than worried. I want to live a life of passion and adventure, to embrace it with all my heart.

I like how bestselling author, speaker, and world-class athlete Dean Karnazes puts it. He says, *"Life is not a journey to the grave with the intention of arriving safely in a pretty and well preserved body, but rather to skid in broadside, thoroughly used up, totally worn out, and loudly proclaiming 'Wow! What a ride!'"* Remember, life is more like a bobsled run than a roller coaster ride. There are no safety rails, but it can still be one hell of a ride! Living life courageously and passionately, as an adventure, with childlike wonder, is how we get the most out of the ride of life. Bring on another chapter!

So far in this book we've talked about finding the courage to live passionately from our core selves. We've talked about growing courage through doing courageous acts, both big and small. We've seen the power that comes from taking action and then executing. We've talked about uncovering our inner passions, and now about living passionately while approaching life as an adventure. These are all more than just "tips" or "hints." They are attitudes and actions that can help sustain us through whatever life brings our way. Now, as this book comes to an end, there are a few closing ideas that I'd like to leave with you. I believe they are essential to being able to follow through on a passionate and courageous existence.

When we are living life passionately, **it's not always about the money**. At the end of the day, having more money will not compensate for the loss of passion. When I tried out for the bobsled team it wasn't about money. It was about being true to me. It wasn't until the bobsledding adventure that I really broke free of the barriers I'd set for myself and began to live passionately. Again, author and speaker Tom Asacker said the following about living passionately as it relates to our present economic state. *"If you've been putting off being passionate about your work in order to make a lot of money, now may be the time for you to make a change. Why? Because the business of making money simply to make more money is quickly coming to an end. The future is* <u>not</u> *in making a buck; it's in making a difference. . . So stop trying to figure it all out. Stop trying to protect yourself from an unknowable future and instead be a connected and passionate part of the here and now."*

It's also important to **challenge your assumptions**. Nothing will put an end to a good idea quicker than false assumptions. If I hadn't challenged my assumptions, you wouldn't be reading this book and I wouldn't be on the speaking circuit. You see, I had worked with a career coach for a few months and during that time, she suggested that I write a book. At the time, I thought that was about the worst idea I had ever heard. Write a book, yeah, right. Where do I sign up . . . not! My impression of authors and speakers was that they were all immensely successful people. CEOs came to mind along with Olympic medalists and superstars. Then, one day, I was watching an author on The Today Show talking about some ridiculous topic he'd written a book about. I'm sure it was a well-written book, but the topic struck me as titillating at best, and shallow at worst. "Maybe I do have something worthwhile to say," I thought. So, I went for it, viewing it as an adventure, and haven't looked back since.

And finally, what separates me from the crowd isn't my native intelligence or my glibness as a writer/speaker, but rather, my willingness to try, sometimes failing, but never feeling like a failure. My life has been about leveling the playing field, not with a world class intellect or a Hall of Fame list of athletic accomplishments, but by a swinging for the fences mentality in whatever I do. There it is. That's my brand. That's what I stand for. I am living proof that the ordinary amongst us can do the extraordinary from time to time. Reveling in that notion is truly what living with courage and passion is all about.

About the Author

In addition to writing, Jim Eschrich is an enlightening and entertaining speaker who addresses a variety of audiences nationwide. He lives with his two girls, Anna and Jamie, and their dog, Nala, in Lenexa, Kansas, a suburb of Kansas City. To contact Jim for speaking or to order books log on to his website at www.couragefortherestofus.com.

BUY A SHARE OF THE FUTURE IN YOUR COMMUNITY

These certificates make great holiday, graduation and birthday gifts that can be personalized with the recipient's name. The cost of one S.H.A.R.E. or one square foot is $54.17. The personalized certificate is suitable for framing and will state the number of shares purchased and the amount of each share, as well as the recipient's name. The home that you participate in "building" will last for many years and will continue to grow in value.

Here is a sample SHARE certificate:

Inside the certificate:

HABITAT FOR HUMANITY

THIS CERTIFIES THAT

YOUR NAME HERE

HAS INVESTED IN A HOME FOR A DESERVING FAMILY

1985-2005

TWENTY YEARS OF BUILDING FUTURES IN OUR COMMUNITY ONE HOME AT A TIME

1200 SQUARE FOOT HOUSE @ $65,000 = $54.17 PER SQUARE FOOT
This certificate represents a tax deductible donation. It has no cash value.

YES, I WOULD LIKE TO HELP!

*I support the work that Habitat for Humanity does and I want to be part of the excitement! As a donor, I will receive periodic updates on your construction activities but, more importantly, I know my gift will help a family in our community realize the dream of homeownership. **I would like to SHARE in your efforts against substandard housing in my community!** (Please print below)*

PLEASE SEND ME _____ SHARES at $54.17 EACH = $ $_____

In Honor Of: _____

Occasion: (Circle One)   HOLIDAY   BIRTHDAY   ANNIVERSARY

OTHER: _____

Address of Recipient: _____

Gift From: _____   *Donor Address:* _____

Donor Email: _____

I AM ENCLOSING A CHECK FOR $ $_____ PAYABLE TO HABITAT FOR HUMANITY <u>OR</u> PLEASE CHARGE MY VISA OR MASTERCARD *(CIRCLE ONE)*

Card Number _____   Expiration Date: _____

Name as it appears on Credit Card _____   Charge Amount $ _____

Signature _____

Billing Address _____

Telephone # Day _____   Eve _____

PLEASE NOTE: Your contribution is tax-deductible to the fullest extent allowed by law.
Habitat for Humanity • P.O. Box 1443 • Newport News, VA 23601 • 757-596-5553
www.HelpHabitatforHumanity.org

Printed in the USA
CPSIA information can be obtained
at www.ICGtesting.com
JSHW082224140824
68134JS00015B/719

9 781600 376870